This book belongs to:

_____

_____

This book is designed to encourage small children to talk about what they see in the colourful pictures. Some simple questions have been suggested, but many more can be made up.

Always try to find a quiet space to share this book with your child. Children will be generous with their responses if you encourage them and give them confidence. They so quickly learn new words and love to use them. A good vocabulary helps them to think and enables them to express their thoughts.

Most importantly, enjoy the book together.

Written by Kath Jewitt
Illustrated by Claire Henley
Language consultant: Betty Root

This edition published by Parragon in 2009

Parragon
Queen Street House
4 Queen Street
Bath BA1 1HE, UK

ISBN 978-1-4054-4448-4
Printed in China

My First Book of...

JUNGLE ANIMALS

Bath · New York · Singapore · Hong Kong · Cologne · Delhi · Melbourne

There are lots of animals in this picture.

Point to all the different animals.

All these animals
live in the jungle.

lion

zebra

snake

elephant

monkey

Say each one's name out loud.

parrot

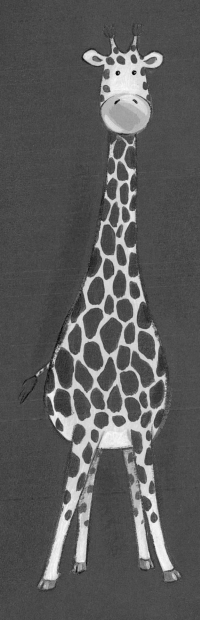

hippopotamus

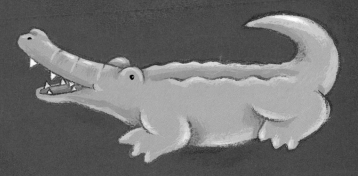

giraffe   crocodile

A daddy lion has long fur round his face, called a mane. Point to the daddy lion.

A mummy lion is called a lioness.
Point to the mummy lion.

A parrot has bright colourful feathers.

Point to a red parrot
in the picture.

Can you find a
blue parrot too?

SNAP! SNAP! These crocodiles have big strong jaws and sharp teeth.

Can you make your arms snap like a crocodile's jaws?

An elephant's nose is called a trunk.

What are these elephants doing?
They are using their trunks
to squirt the water!

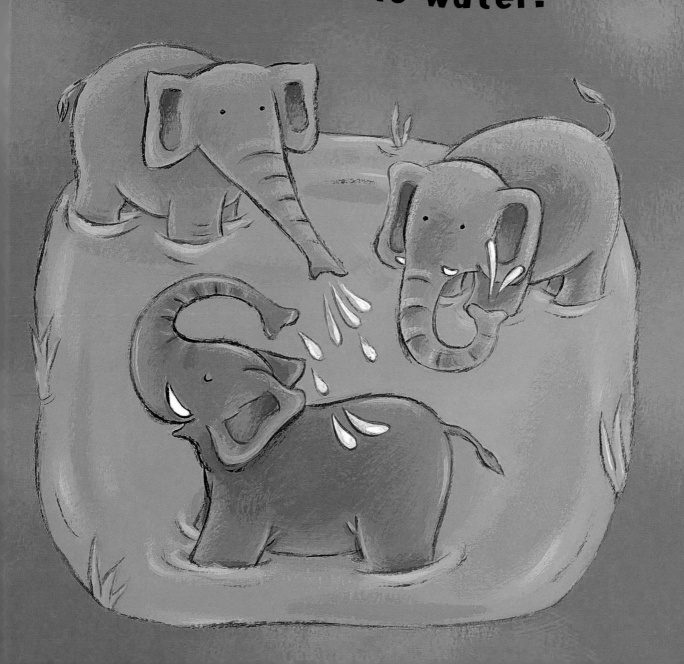

Zebras have lots of black and white stripes.

Can you spot another stripy animal in the picture? Can you find a creature with spots?

These playful monkeys love to jump, swing and climb in the tall trees.

Try to be like
a playful monkey.

Giraffes have long necks and legs, to help them reach the leaves on the trees.

Pretend to be a tall giraffe.
Stretch up as high as you can.

Snakes have no arms or legs.
They slide and slither along.

How many snakes can you spot in this picture? Point to each one.

Hippopotamuses are very big.
This hippo is bathing
in the pool to keep cool.

Point to a small creature in the picture.

Can you make a noise like each of these jungle animals?

roar!

squawk!

terrummp!

Make each noise
as loudly as you can!

hiss!

oo, oo!

snap!

Which jungle animal
is your favourite?